INDIGENOUS AMERICAN CULTURES

Celebrating the CHINOOK Tribes

ANNE ACCARDI

Mitchell Lane
PUBLISHERS

Parent and Caregiver Tips for Creating Nonfiction Readers

The high-interest topics in the ***Indigenous American Cultures*** series are sure to get your young reader excited about reading nonfiction. While exploring a fascinating subject, your reader will be introduced to new facts, ideas, and vocabulary.

Tips for Reading Nonfiction

Talk about Nonfiction

Explain that nonfiction books provide facts about real-world topics. When readers read nonfiction, they gain a rich understanding of the world. They build background knowledge that provides a foundation for learning and academic success.

Look at the Parts

This book contains the following helpful features. Share the purpose of each feature with your reader.

Photos, Captions, and Graphic Aids
The photos, captions, maps, diagrams, time lines, and other graphic aids in nonfiction texts contain a wealth of information. Help your reader identify different ways information can be displayed.

Sidebars
These extra tidbits of information help satisfy readers' curiosity and expand their knowledge.

Table of Contents
Located at the front of the book, this list shows the big ideas within the text and the page numbers where they can be found.

Glossary
Located at the back of the book, the glossary defines key words and phrases that are related to the topic. These words and phrases can be found in the text in colored type.

Comprehension Questions (Fact Check)
Multiple-choice questions help readers self-check to make sure they understand what they read.

Index
Located at the back of the book, the index is an alphabetical list of topics and the page numbers where they can be found.

With a little help and guidance, your reader will be on their way to enjoying and learning from nonfiction books.

Mitchell Lane
PUBLISHERS
mitchelllanepub.com

2001 SW 31st Avenue
Hallandale, FL 33009

First Edition, 2026.
Author: Anne Accardi
Designer: Rhea Magaro
Editor: Kim Thompson

Series: Indigenous American Cultures
Title: Celebrating the Chinook Tribes / by Anne Accardi

Hallandale, FL : Mitchell Lane Publishers, [2026]

Library bound ISBN: 979-8-89260-552-6
Paperback ISBN: 979-8-89260-588-5
eBook ISBN: 979-8-89260-561-8

PHOTO CREDITS
Alamy: Danita Delimont, cover, 1; Heritage Image Partnership Ltd, 5; Classic Image, 8; Ian Dewar, 10; NadyZima_Klgd, 12; Brian Jaansen, 13; North Wind Pictures Archive, 15; Danita Delimont, 19, 25; Zuma Press, 21, 22; Peter Horree, 28; James anderson, 29; Dreamstime: Clovercity, cover, 1; Public Domain: Chinook Nation, 6; TouchUp7.0, 7; Wiki, 9, 14, 16, 18, 20, 25, 26; Chinook Indian Nation and Ridgeland Wildlife Refuge, 15; NOAA, 23; LOC, 24; Shutterstock: Bob Pool, cover, 1, 7; Jim Cottingham, cover, 1; lilik ferri yanto, 4; WildWestScott, 11; Spiz Photography, 27

CONTENTS

A CHINOOK CONNECTION

Have you ever eaten salmon fresh off the grill? If you have, you enjoyed the same wild food that has fed the Chinook people for thousands of years.

Long ago, tens of thousands of these **Indigenous** Americans lived in the region where the Pacific Ocean meets the Columbia River. Each year, the Chinook people waited for the **salmon run** that allowed them to catch their favorite food. One kind of salmon, the highly-prized Chinook salmon, is named after them.

CHINOOK HISTORY

For thousands of years, the Chinook were a powerful group of tribes in the Pacific Northwest. Their homeland is now part of Oregon and Washington.

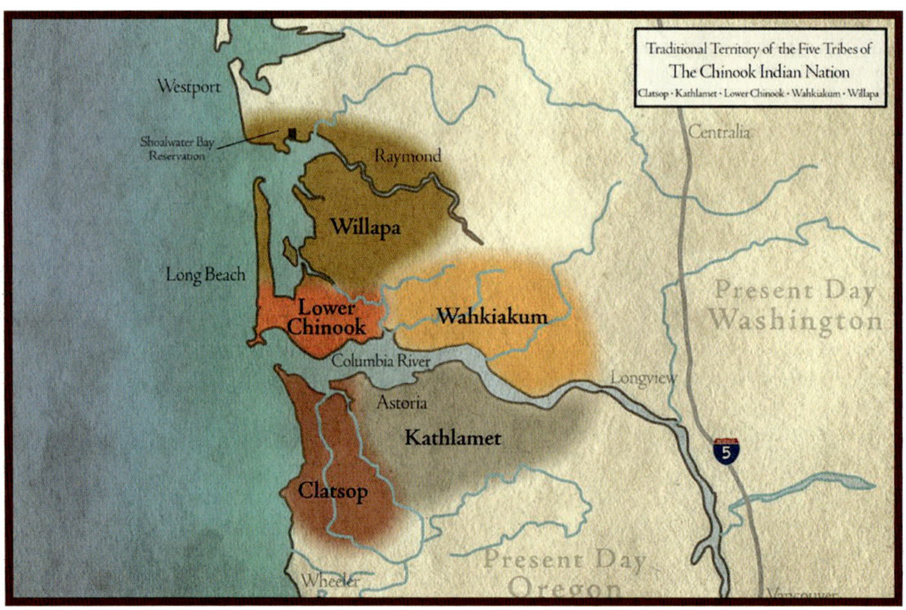

The Chinook were experts at traveling on the Columbia River and other waterways. They were also very successful traders. They traded dried fish, canoes, seashells, furs, and other goods. They visited tribes that lived far away. The Chinook language was known by people in present-day California, Alaska, and Idaho.

European **settlers** arrived on Chinook land in the 1700s. They brought **epidemics** that made Chinook people sick. Many died.

In the 1800s, gold was discovered in the Northwest. The United States government wanted control of Chinook lands. They forced Chinook tribes to move. The people were not allowed to hunt or fish in their homeland.

Culture Close-Up

The American explorers Lewis and Clark and their expedition met the Chinook in 1805. This painting is called *Lewis and Clark on the Lower Columbia*. It shows the first encounter between the two groups.

Today, the Chinook Nation is made up of five tribes. They include the Willapa, Wahkiakum, Lower Chinook, Kathlamet, and Clatsop. There are approximately 3,000 members who live mostly in Washington and Oregon. There are also other Chinook tribes. People with Chinook **ancestry** live throughout the U.S.

For a long time, the Chinook have asked the U.S. government to let them be a **sovereign** nation. But the government still does not recognize the Chinook Nation.

The Confederated Tribes of Siletz Indians include Indigenous peoples from throughout the Pacific Northwest.

Culture Close-Up

A Chinook is a strong wind that sometimes brings warm, dry air over the Rocky Mountains. It is named after the Chinook people because they were among the first to recognize it. They called it the "Snow Eater." The CH-47 *Chinook* is a U.S. military helicopter. It is named for this wind and for the Chinook people.

EXPLORING CHINOOK PLACES

To learn more about the Chinook, you can visit Tansy Point in Oregon. The site has beautiful views of the Columbia River.

Here, Chinook and U.S. leaders met in 1851. They signed **treaties** that would allow the Chinook to stay in their homeland. But the Tansy Point Treaties were never approved by the U.S. government. The Chinook Nation wants to reclaim Tansy Point and build a cultural center there.

tansy plant

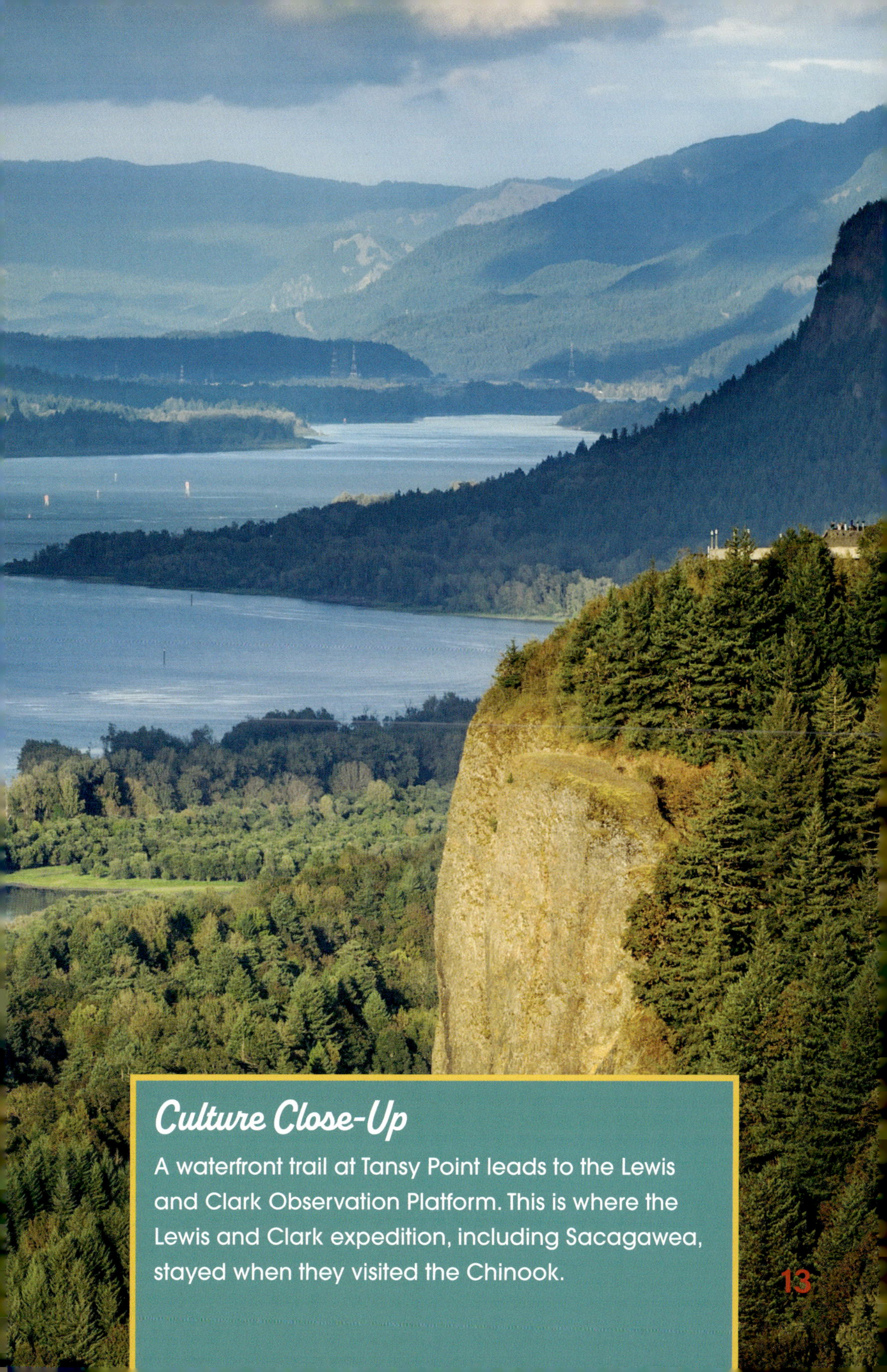

Culture Close-Up

A waterfront trail at Tansy Point leads to the Lewis and Clark Observation Platform. This is where the Lewis and Clark expedition, including Sacagawea, stayed when they visited the Chinook.

You can also find out about the Chinook at the Cathlapotle Plankhouse in Washington. It stands on the site of Cathlapotle, a large Chinook town founded in 1450.

Culture Close-Up

To get into a traditional Chinook plankhouse, you had to duck through the small circular door. You may have been required to leave your weapons outside.

The rebuilt house shows how the Chinook lived long ago. It has sleeping benches and fire pits. Visitors can walk inside to learn about the relationship the Chinook had with local plants and animals. The building is used for modern Chinook events like the Winter Gathering.

THE CHINOOK LANGUAGE

As the Chinook traded with people all along the Pacific coast, they helped spread a trading language. It combined Chinook words with words from other tribes, French, and English. The language is called Chinuk Wawa, Chinook Talk, or Chinook Jargon.

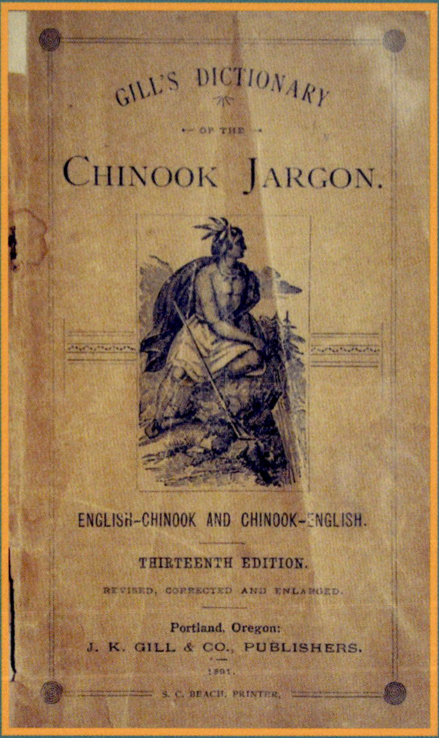

By the 1990s, only a few people spoke Chinuk Wawa. But now, more people are learning. They sign up for community classes or study Chinuk Wawa in college. A free app helps people learn the language.

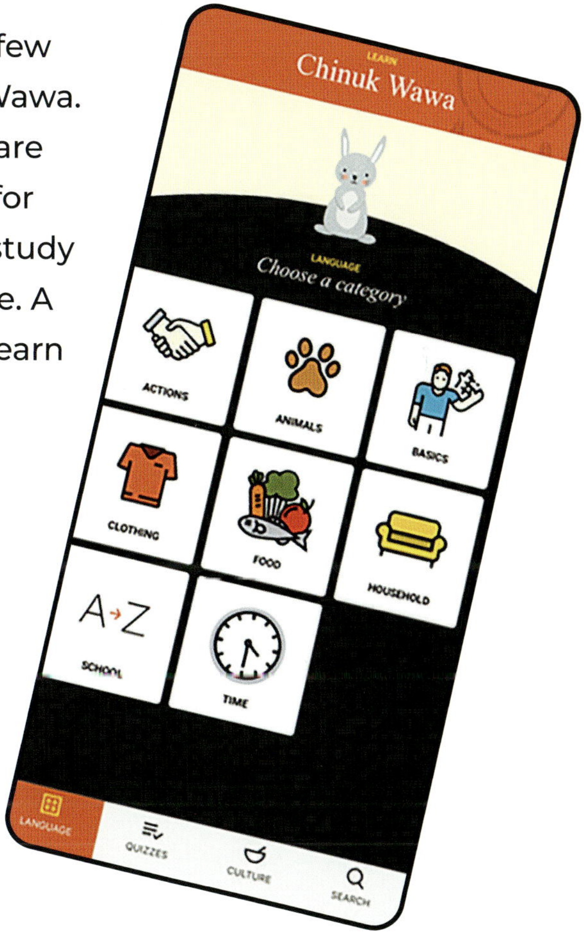

Culture Close-Up

Practice these Chinuk Wawa words and phrases.

Lush san. (Good day.)

laxayam (hello or goodbye)

nayka nim (my name is)

qHata (how are you?)

Masi. (Thank you.)

HONORING CHINOOK TRADITIONS

Long ago, Chinook artists used wood, bone, stone, antler, and horn. They made spoons, bowls, pipes, and canoes. They carved symbols into the objects to give them power.

Tsin'is'tum may have been the last full-blooded member of the Clatsop tribe. She was known for her basketwork. She died in 1905.

Chinook baskets are valuable collector's items. Traditionally, the waterproof baskets carried food and other goods during travel on rivers.

Today, Chinook artists carry on the tradition. Like their ancestors, they weave baskets from pieces of roots, twigs, and bark that are dried and dyed.

Since ancient times, the Chinook have held potlatches. In the Chinuk Wawa language, *potlatch* means "to give." Chinook families hosted other families on special occasions. They served a feast and gave away their possessions to guests. They gave blankets, tools, furs, weapons, and other valuable items.

Chinook people still hold potlatches. Tribes give generous gifts when they host other tribes for celebrations.

CHINOOK CELEBRATIONS

Salmon are **sacred** to the Chinook. For generations, the start of the salmon run each spring has been celebrated with the First Salmon Ceremony. Traditionally, one hunter is chosen to catch the first salmon. The fish is cooked carefully. Its bones are returned to the river. The ceremony shows respect for salmon so that they keep coming back each year.

The Chinook still celebrate the First Salmon Ceremony. In 2024, it was held at Tansy Point. The first salmon was carried on cedar sticks and cooked over an outdoor fire. Kids put berries in the first fish's mouth to honor the animal and bring about a good catch.

A boy carries a toy salmon on sticks during a First Salmon Ceremony. The ceremony honors the First Food that has fed the Chinook for generations.

The Chinook have traveled by canoe for thousands of years. Some of their traditional canoes could hold more than 30 people. Holes in the sides made them lighter and easier to carry over land.

Today, the Chinook participate in Canoe Journey. The event began in 1989. Each year, a different Indigenous nation hosts. Teams paddle to visit the host tribe. They make stops to pick up more teams. At each stop, teams sing and dance for their hosts. At the end, the host tribe sings and dances. They present gifts at a potlatch.

FAMOUS FACES

J. Christopher Stevens was a U.S. **ambassador** and member of the Chinook Nation. He worked for peace in the Middle East. Sadly, he died in 2012 during a violent attack in the country of Libya.

Catherine Herrold Troeh was a nurse who spent her life helping the Chinook people. She was the only woman to join the Chinook Tribal Council when it formed in 1952.

Both Stevens and Troeh were related to Chief Comcomly. This respected Chinook leader welcomed the explorers Lewis and Clark. Comcomly was known for his skill in business and trade. A legend says that Lewis and Clark tried to bargain with Comcomly for his coat made of sea otter fur.

Culture Close-Up

Traditionally, the Chinook buried their dead in canoes that were raised above the ground. This statue overlooking the Columbia River is shaped like a burial canoe. It honors the great Chief Comcomly.

LESSONS FROM THE CHINOOK

The Chinook people are made up of many tribes. They believe in working together. They want to care for the land that has taken care of them for thousands of years.

Today, the Chinook are still fighting to be recognized by the U.S. They celebrate their culture and honor their **heritage**. Learning about Chinook traditions can help all Americans learn to respect each other.

Chinook people gathered at the Chinook Indian Nation rally in Seattle, Washington. They called for the U.S. government to grant them the same rights as other Indigenous American tribes.

GLOSSARY

ambassador (am-BAS-uh-dur): a government official who lives and works in another country

ancestry (AN-ces-tree): belonging to a line of family members who came before you; your ancestors

epidemics (ep-i-DEM-iks): outbreaks of diseases that affect many people at once

heritage (HER-i-tij): traditions and beliefs that people consider to be an important part of their history

Indigenous (in-DI-juh-nuhs): the earliest known inhabitants of a place

sacred (SAY-krid): holy, very important, and deserving of great respect

salmon run (SAM-uhn run): an annual migration where salmon swim from the ocean into freshwater rivers and streams to lay eggs

settlers (SET-luhrz): people who make their homes in a new place and who have historically invaded and oppressed Indigenous peoples who originally lived there

sovereign (SAHV-ruhn): independent and self-ruling; having power

treaties (TREE-tees): agreements between two or more nations

FACT CHECK

1. How many tribes make up Chinook Nation?

   A. three B. five C. seven

2. For thousands of years, the Chinook have lived in the _____.

   A. Great Plains B. Eastern Atlantic C. Pacific Northwest

3. The Chinuk Wawa language was developed for _______.

   A. trading B. fishing C. potlatches

4. Tansy Point overlooks _________.

   A. the Columbia River B. the city of Seattle C. Idaho

Answers: 1. B, 2. C, 3. A, 4. A

FURTHER READING

Caswell, Max. *My Life in a Chinook Village*. Gareth Stevens, 2017.

Weso, Tom Pecore. *Native American Stories for Kids: 12 Traditional Stories from Indigenous Tribes across North America*. Callisto Kids, 2022.

Yasuda, Anita. *Native Nations of the Northwest Coast*. The Child's World, Inc., 2011.

ON THE INTERNET

Chinook Nation
chinooknation.org
Explore this official site to learn about Chinook history and culture.

Discover Lewis & Clark: Chinookan Peoples
lewis-clark.org/native-nations/chinookan-peoples
This site has articles and resources about the Chinookan people

Native American Hall of Fame
nativehalloffame.org
Find biographies of well-known Native Americans from the 1860s to the present.

INDEX

ABOUT THE AUTHOR

Anne Accardi is an author from Kansas City, Missouri. She is thrilled to share facts about Indigenous Americans with young people. She loves history and finding ways to connect the past with the present and future. When she's not reading or writing, you can find Anne in a library, museum, or movie theater.